instead of the mag-
neto call, the connec-
tion is to be made with
a push button, and is
a thoroughly reliable
instrument.
Price with case com-
plete as shown in cut,
made of oak or black
walnut.
Each $7.00

one, same style as above, but
ls included. Each....... $16.50

No. 6314. Transmitter,
long distance with granu-
lated carbon; can be at-
tached to telephones of any
make on which the trans-
mitter is not satisfactory or
has given out, same as used
on our improved long dis-
tance telephones, but made
to screw on the front of the
box; is very easily attached.
Price $2.00

No. 6315.

itches for small telephone ex-
ons or over.
...................................20c

ENTERTAINMENT OR EX-
ION OUTFIT.

he Entertainment or Exhibi-
f the following pieces:
lking machine and oak carrying
liaphragm, one automatic extra
phragm, one speaking tube, one
crew driver, complete.... $25.00
g Records, your own se-

hree persons............... 6.00
.... 3.00
cert work.................. 1.00

---

dered paper from
large clear type,
bound in extra
silk finish cloth,
stamped in gold,
uniform with Les
Miserables, aver-
aging 600 pages to
the vol.
Publishers' price
.... $2.50
Our price. 1.00
Postage extra 30c

**52216. Hugo's
Works, com-
plete in 7 Vols.**
Library edition
printed on cal-
endered paper
from new plates
made from long
primer type,
averaging 650
pages to the vol.
bound in extra
cloth, stamped in gold, gilt top, containing 14 full
page inserted illustrations, printed on plate paper.
Publishers' price..$8.75   Our price......$4.25

**52218. George
Eliot's Works.**
Printed from
clear type on
fine quality pa-
per, illustrated,
durably bound
in heavy cloth,
complete 8 vols.

Publishers' price................................. $6.00
Our price.. $3.25
Cheaper edition, in 6 vols, 12 mo., size uniform.
Publishers' price..$4.50   Our price......$2.65
52220. Opie Read's Works.
Substantially and neatly
bound in extra cloth, gilt
top, printed on fine paper
from clear type, 5 vols.
Per set........... $3.20
Separately per vol. .75c
Postage each extra 12c
My Young Master.
The Jucklins.
The Kentucky Colonel.
The Tennesee Judge.
On The Swanee River.

52222. Emerson's Essays.
Two volumes, complete, sub-
stantially and attractively
bound in binder's silk cloth,
12mo. size in neat box.
Publisher's price..... $0.75
Our price.............. .40
Postage extra, 24c.
52224. Samuel Smile's Works.
Attractively bound in English
silk cloth, gilt top, printed
from clear type on fine paper,
12mo. uniform, 4 volumes.
Duty.   Thrift.   Character.   Self-Help.
Publisher's price ..$1.75   Our price. $1.10
Postage extra, 45c.
Separately, per volume.................. .30
Postage each extra 12c

**52234.   J.
Fennimore
Cooper's Works.** Leather
Stocking Tales, Illus-
trated. Large, clear type
edition, printed on fine
paper from clear type,
each volume containing
from 400 to 450 pages. The
volumes are very durably
bound in binder's silk fin-
ish cloth. Contents of the
five volumes as follows:
The Deerslayer.
The Pathfinder.
The Prairie.
The Pioneers.
The Last of the Mohicans.
Publisher's price................. $3.75
Our price........................ 1.00
Postage extra 5c.

[barcode] MW00958389

ments. If, however, there
is anything special that is wanted kindly advise us and
we shall be glad to make quotations. Our prices will
be found to be far lower than the manufacturers, and
we believe that a trial order placed with us for anything that may be needed in this line will convince the
purchaser that we can save him much money and that
we shall be able to merit his future patronage. In addition to our Learner's Instrument, we wish to call
special attention to the fact that we list the high
grade Standard Western Union instruments, which
need no further recommendation.

TERMS OF SHIPMENT.

Electrical goods will be sent by express C. O. D.
when desired, providing $1.00 accompanies the order as
a guarantee of good faith. The balance can be paid at
the express office after examination.
It is best to send cash in full with your order and
save the discount of 3 per cent. also return express
charges on money.

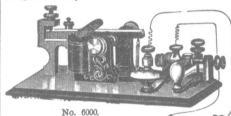

No. 6000.

No. 6000. Learner's Outfit, complete, for telegraphy, consisting
of full size sounder and key,
mounted on polished cherry base;
has full sized battery, with wire,
chemicals and complete book of instructions, with everything necessary for operating for private practice, complete weight about 10½ lbs.
Price..................................... $3.00
No. 6001. Learner's Instrument,
same as above, without battery,
weight about 2 pounds. Each...................... $2.25
No. 6002. Learner's Instrument, mounted on base,
as above, but has sounder wound to 20 ohms. for long
distance and should be used on line of ¼ mile or more,
as it will give better results, weight 2 pounds.
Each...................................... $2.90
No. 6006. Private Line Instrument, the highest
grade, made with steel lever, key and tubular sounder,
same style as Western Union, but one size smaller, on
polished cherry wood base, with polished rubber covered coils, wound to 20 ohms resistance. Each.. $3.90

No. 6009.

No. 6008. Steel Lever Key. Standard Western
Union, with legs to go through the table. These keys
are of the latest and most improved type, the lever
and trunions being made of solid steel, nickel plated,
instead of brass, as in the old type of instrument. The
same strength is secured with much lighter weight and
the liability of loose trunions completely avoided. This
is without doubt one of the most handsome and best

---

es
ated
: finis
ublis
ur pr

2.
ht w
m la
fume
cloth, st
page ins
as follow
Edmund
Twenty
Louise I
The Son
Publis
Our pr

52234.
Cooper's
Stocking
trated.
edition,
paper
each vo
from 400
volumes
bound in
ish cloth
five volu
The Dee
The Pat
The Pra
The Pio
The Las
Publis
Our pr

52236.
binder's
paper fr
ing:
Wat
Red
Publis

book orde
count for
52242. T
This new
such of
recitati
proved
tested a
tion of
elocutio
and Eur
orignial
there ar
ious sel
be found
ation.
tions, "
Hur.
The Flo

LIFE IN AMERICA 100 YEARS AGO

Communication

LIFE IN AMERICA 100 YEARS AGO

Communication

Geraldine Gan

Chelsea House Publishers
Philadelphia

CHELSEA HOUSE PUBLISHERS
Editorial Director: Richard Rennert
Production Manager: Pamela Loos
Art Director: Sara Davis
Picture Editor: Judy Hasday
Senior Production Editor: Lisa Chippendale

LIFE IN AMERICA 100 YEARS AGO
Senior Editor: John Ziff

Staff for **COMMUNICATION**
Associate Editor: Therese De Angelis
Editorial Assistant: Kristine Brennan
Designer: Terry Mallon
Picture Researcher: Sandy Jones
Cover Illustration: Robert Gerson

3 5 7 9 8 6 4 2
Library of Congress Cataloging-in-Publication Data
Gan, Geraldine.
    Communication / Geraldine M. Gan.
            p. cm. — (Life in America 100 years ago)
    Includes bibliographical references and index.
    ISBN 0-7910-2845-3 (hc)
    1. Communication—United States—History—19th century. I. Title. II. Series.

P92.U5G36 1997   96-53516
302.2'0973'09034—dc21   CIP
                                                                              AC

CONTENTS

LIFE IN AMERICA 100 YEARS AGO

Communication

Education

Frontier Life

Government and Politics

Health and Medicine

Industry and Business

Law and Order

Manners and Customs

Sports and Recreation

Transportation

Urban Life

Communication

The Postal Service

THE SIMPLEST AND MOST DIRECT WAY FOR TWO PEOPLE TO communicate with each other is to talk face-to-face. Obviously, though, that method only works when the individuals are in close proximity. From colonial days until the middle of the 19th century, sending letters through the mail was the only means of long-distance communication available to Americans. Yet for over 200 years the mails were slow and unreliable. Several factors contributed to the growth of the United States Postal Service during the 19th century: improved transportation, mechanization, reforms in postage rates and rules, and upgraded working conditions for postal workers.

THE BEGINNING

In early colonial America, most mail traveled overseas between the colonies and the British isles. The first American "post offices" were actually taverns or coffeehouses where mail was collected in a bag to be sent overseas on a merchant ship. The captain of the ship would collect a penny for each piece of mail taken aboard.

Communication

While today's Post Office is highly regulated, during the 19th century it relied on the grit and independence of carriers such as this gentleman on his mule-drawn cart.

In 1672, the first overland postal service was established between New York and Boston, and other intercity routes followed. As the population grew, so did the need for postal services. The first courier service, which depended on horseback riders, was established between Portsmouth, New Hampshire, and Philadelphia, Pennsylvania, in 1693. By 1763, routes connected two more colonial cities, as well as two cities in Canada.

After the Revolution, post offices and post roads were established in accordance with the Constitution of 1789. Congress created the United States Post Office as a part of the federal government and appointed Samuel Osgood of Massachusetts as the first postmaster general. By the end of the 18th century, the United States had set up nearly 400 post offices and mapped out 12,000 miles of postal routes. Postal rates, which were calculated on the basis of distance traveled, tended to be high. It cost 25 cents to mail a one-page letter more than 400 miles—a considerable expense in the early 19th century. Furthermore, people had to pay their carriers two cents upon receipt of mail.

As the United States continued to expand, mail services tried to keep pace. After the purchase of Alaska from Russia in 1867, steamships delivered mail to this icy, rugged land, since there were no accessible postal routes. Postal improvements proceeded slowly in Alaska until gold was discovered in Juneau during the 1880s; by 1890, Alaska's prospectors were receiving mail regularly—by dogsled. The annexation of Hawaii in 1898 presented fewer challenges, since the islands already had their own mail delivery system, which was quickly incorporated into the mainland system. Mail began to reach foreign destinations more efficiently; the Universal Postal Union was established in 1878 to standardize international mailing rates for its member nations. By 1885, 54 countries had joined, and that number had increased to 71 by 1906.

As the 1800s drew to a close, America's mail delivery system was beginning to resemble the one that we enjoy today. In 1890, there were 62,401 post offices being served by half a million miles of mail routes. Through all methods of delivery, the mails were traveling a total of 327 million miles a year, and more than 150,000 postal workers were handling about 8,000 letters a minute. The Post Office Department's goal at the time, according to Postmaster General John Wanamaker, was "to make the mails go faster, more safely, and more frequently"

THE PONY EXPRESS

Although it remains forever a part of the Wild West's romantic mythology, the Pony Express was actually a financial failure that ran only for about 16 months. It was a fast overland mail service using relays of horseback riders to carry urgent messages between St. Joseph, Missouri and Sacramento, California. The private firm of Russell, Majors, and Waddell founded the Pony Express, investing nearly half a million dollars in 190 stations, 500 horses, and 80 intrepid young riders.

Pony Express riders had to be courageous: their route followed established stagecoach paths as far as Salt Lake City, Utah, but after that, they headed west through the punishing deserts of Utah and Nevada to reach California. They galloped through summer heat, winter blizzards, packs of wolves and prides of mountain lions, and attacks by Native Americans angered by further invasion of the West. It was Pony Express riders who informed the western states of President Lincoln's election in 1860, carrying the news from Fort Kearny, Nebraska, to Fort Churchill, Nevada, in a mere six days.

An advertisement for Pony Express service in New York City. The Express employed intrepid riders to carry mail from coast to coast in 10 short days. The enterprise went under after less than two years of operation, however. The high cost of sending mail (at the time of this 1861 ad, one dollar per half ounce) was one reason for its demise.

Even this amazing feat, however, could not keep the Pony Express alive. At one dollar per half ounce, Pony Express mail was very expensive to send. Furthermore, with the Civil War threatening to begin at any time, officials in Washington wanted to keep the western states involved in American affairs. Therefore, communication had to be faster. Western Union answered this need by establishing a transcontinental telegraph line in late 1861. These factors all contributed to the demise of the Pony Express—at a loss of almost half of its investors' money.

TRANSPORTATION

Bold experiments such as the Pony Express were part of the trial-and-error process of finding effective ways to move mail from place to place. The Railway Mail Service, founded in 1863, was perhaps the most important postal innovation of the Civil War period. RPOs, or railway post offices, were up and running by 1874 on the Chicago and Northwestern Railroad, where they enabled mail to be picked up and sorted in transit, rather than taken to a conventional post office for sorting. The railway cars speeded transcontinental delivery tremendously; coast-to-coast mail service by RPO car took just 7 days, as opposed to 16 to 20 days by stagecoach. Railway mail service also made delivery by steamboat obsolete, since trains could now reach remote towns. Railroad routes spanned 67,734 miles in 1874—more than double what they had been in the previous decade.

One special type of Railway Mail Service vehicle, the Fast Mail train, could get 33 tons of mail from New York to St. Louis in less than a day and a half. Despite their remarkable speed, the Fast Mail trains were halted in July of 1876, having been in service for a mere 10 months. The Post Office cited budget reductions as the reason for their cancellation, but reinstated Fast Mail trains in 1881. This time, they served additional cities and service was upgraded so much that by 1889, mail went from

Curious onlookers study one of the Postal Department's three-wheeled mail trucks, introduced in 1913. A single truck did the work of three mail carriers on horseback.

New York to San Francisco in only four and a half days. The revitalized Fast Mail trains received public acclaim for their speedy service and even earned mention in songs and poems of the time as romanticized symbols of American ingenuity.

In 1891, the Post Office experimented with mail delivery by electric cable car in St. Louis. By 1895, the Railway Mail Service had 12 streetcar lines running in six major cities. One year later, 26 streetcar lines operated in 15 cities.

Another Post Office experiment was the pneumatic tube line, first used in 1893 to deliver large volumes of mail in Philadelphia. This network of underground tubes was fast; sending mail half a mile through them took less than 2 minutes, as opposed to the 15 required by a horse-drawn postal wagon. As Philadelphia's pneumatic tube line branched out, Boston and New York completed similar systems in 1898. Each pneumatic tube carrier was about 21 inches long and 7 inches in diameter and could hold about 600 letters. More than 350,000 letters per hour could travel down the lines.

In congested cities, the system was far more efficient than wagon or streetcar delivery. The cost of building and maintaining pneumatic tube routes was deemed excessive, however, and the service was suspended in 1901. Although pneumatic tube service was reinstated the following year, debates about its cost-efficiency raged on until the Post Office officially terminated it in 1953.

The "horseless wagon" would soon outmode most other forms of mail transport. In 1899, both Cleveland and Buffalo experimented with automobile delivery routes. By 1911, postal trucks were handling mail delivery in at least nine major cities—with one truck handling the work once done by three carriers on horseback. It wasn't until 1918, however, that postal trucks were a common sight throughout World War I America.

This mass of cranks and gears was the first postmarking and canceling machine deemed acceptable for use in post offices. Designed by Thomas and Martin Leavitt of Boston and patented in 1879, it could process mail nearly eight times faster than a postal clerk could manually.

MECHANIZATION

As transportation improved, mail moved with increasing speed, and the country's growing population meant that the volume of mail also increased annually. In 1886, for instance, the Post Office delivered nearly 4 billion pieces of mail throughout the United States and its territories; in 1895, that number reached 5 billion. How, then, could mail sorters and handlers keep up with what was fast becoming an avalanche of letters?

Postmarking and canceling stamps seemed like simple tasks, but the mechanization of these activities saved postal workers a great deal of time, since they could now be performed in a single step. At least five patents for mechanical canceling machines were issued between 1868 and 1874, but none of these designs was accepted by the U.S. Post Office. In 1876, Thomas and Martin Leavitt of Boston patented a design that met with the government's approval. In fact, the Leavitts' Number 3 machine, invented in 1882, was the only model accepted by Congress for use in post offices. It could cancel and postmark 15,000 letters per hour, whereas the average postal clerk could process only 2,000 by hand.

The development of machinery to postmark mail was helpful not only from the standpoint of speed; it also helped ensure that no mail went unmarked because of human error. In 1897, First Assistant Postmaster General Heath pointed out the importance of uniform postmarking, stating that accurately dated mail was vital "as evidence before the courts, in business transactions conducted through the mails, and in fixing the responsibility where mail has been improperly handled by postal officials." By 1910, a number of different models of canceling machines had been approved by the U.S. Post Office, which had more than 2,172 machines operating nationwide.

POSTAL REFORMS

As the postal service extended its geographic reach to serve more Americans, it also became more difficult to regulate. As early as 1753–1774, when Benjamin Franklin served as England's first deputy postmaster to the colonies, it was necessary to enact reforms. His administration greatly improved colonial postal services, enforcing shorter routes, faster delivery by stagecoach, nighttime runs in the North, direct service between England and the South, and regularly scheduled service between England and North America.

Benjamin Franklin, inventor, statesman, scientist, essayist, and publisher, served as deputy postmaster to the 13 original colonies from 1753 to 1774.

In 1847, Congress began authorizing postal reforms recommended by Rowland Hill, an English educator whose suggestions had already been enacted in England by 1840. The United States gradually implemented his ideas, including the practice of selling prepaid, glue-backed stamps and the establishment of uniform postage rates that were not based on distance traveled. In 1863, postage rates were set at three cents for a half-ounce letter, and three separate classes of mail were defined, which included special rates for books and newspapers. "Free delivery" was enacted in 49 American cities. This meant that residents in urban centers did not have to report to a post office to send or receive mail because carriers would pick up and deliver at their residential mailboxes. During the first quarter under this new system, nearly 4 million pieces of mail were delivered—an increase of about 25 percent from the previous quarter.

Expanded services like free delivery meant that postal carriers had to work harder, prompting Postmaster General Alexander W. Randall to plead for better wages on their behalf, noting that they "travel every day early in the morning until late at night, in heat and cold and rain and snow. . . ." In 1866, compensation for mail carriers increased as a result of Randall's appeal. The number of carriers grew steadily throughout this period; by 1890, 9,066 carriers were employed by 454 post offices.

In 1873, Postmaster General John Creswell borrowed the Austrian idea of postal cards in an effort to contain the cost of sending nonconfidential mail. At just a penny each, postal cards caught on quickly; more than 64 million were mailed in their first year of use, and the total reached almost 273 million by 1880. The price of "private mailing cards" was still one cent in 1898—a rate that held steady until 1952.

Regular mail, too, underwent changes. The postage rate for regular mail was reduced from three to two cents for a half-ounce letter in 1883. It dropped again in 1885 to two cents for a full ounce—and did not change until 1932.

Creswell not only lowered the cost of sending mail for the average American, but he also questioned the right of government officials to send mail for free. He suspended this privilege (called franking) in 1873, forcing government agencies to purchase special stamps and

This man enjoys the benefits of rural free delivery service, which eliminated the need to travel to remote post offices and pay postage fees to get regular mail. When Postmaster General John Wanamaker successfully established rural free delivery (RFD) in 1896, he put rural Americans on equal footing with "city folk," who already had free delivery.

envelopes with federal funds. The Post Office Department benefited from this new source of revenue, but the reform was short-lived. In 1877, government officeholders were permitted to frank documents if the words "Official Business" appeared on their envelopes. After this decision, Creswell's reform steadily weakened until franking was as prevalent as it had been before 1873.

One area of the country's mail system that had not seen much reform since colonial times was rural delivery service. This was an especially noticeable inadequacy, since more than half of the population (76 million in 1890) lived in remote hamlets. Free delivery service, which benefited just one quarter of all Americans, was available only in cities. Not only did millions of farmers have to travel long distances to reach the nearest post offices, but they also had to pay postage upon receipt of mail. Many perceived themselves as footing the $11 million bill that made free delivery possible for "city folk."

Postmaster General John Wanamaker attempted to start rural free delivery (RFD) in 1891 with little success. His second attempt, in 1896, yielded much better results. Farmers could collect newspapers, magazines, and letters daily from their roadside mailboxes, resulting in a better-informed public. By 1899, RFD was operating in 41 states; by 1902, there were 8,298 rural mail service routes. Large postal wagons, inspired by the "traveling post office system" of the Railway Mail Service, navigated these routes. The wagons held two postal workers who could receive, postmark, and sort mail en route. In 1906, the RFD system was streamlined even more when carriers who had automobiles were allowed to use them on the job.

One consequence of RFD implementation was an effort to improve country roads. Between 1897 and 1908, rural districts scrambled to meet the road standards set by the Post Office Department. The necessary road upgrades cost about $72 million in all.

Before 1910, postal workers had no guarantee of fair treatment—or even of a safe work environment with serviceable equipment. After that year's reforms, however, workers' hours were regulated, buildings were renovated, and even such seemingly minute details as keeping mailbags in good repair were attended to.

As more people received pieces of identical mail, such as newspapers and magazines, the Post Office tried to deal with mass mailings as efficiently as possible. The introduction of "precanceled" stamps to denote prepayment was a partial solution. By 1904, however, precanceled stamps were rendered unnecessary when a new policy allowed mass mailings of 2,000 or more items to be delivered when marked with a permit number that indicated prepayment of postage. This practice, known as "permit mailing," is still used for all kinds of bulk commercial mailings.

23

WORKING CONDITIONS

Even with advances in transportation, machines to handle the most tedious tasks, and codified rates that eliminated guesswork, postal employees of a century ago often found themselves in a taxing—sometimes dangerous—occupation. In 1893, a mail clerk in a major city like Chicago might handle up to 312,500 pieces of mail a year and work 10- or 12-hour days, including Sundays and holidays. The safety of working conditions was left to chance: while some post offices were housed in federal buildings, many were leased on commercial property and in dire need of renovation.

In turn-of-the-century New York, conditions in post office buildings bordered on the inhumane. One New York City clerk described the atmosphere as "laden with the most pestilential microbes brought by the sacks containing the mail matter, besides the most vile stenches which prevail for want of proper ventilation."

In 1910 the government implemented a long-overdue policy mandating the construction of buildings for the exclusive use of post offices in major cities. These new buildings were located as close as possible to large railroad stations in order to speed mail on its way. For the convenience of the workers, post offices also began to install conveyor belts to move mail through and even between buildings.

These reforms also provided for the workers' personal well-being. Ventilation systems were added to protect their health, and in 1911, postal workers were given Sundays off and overtime pay for workdays in excess of eight hours.

Books

IN RECENT YEARS BOOKSTORES HAVE EVOLVED INTO spacious, comfortable reading rooms. Some even sell refreshments and host cultural events. Book subscription clubs, having existed in some form for about 300 years, continue to prosper as well. While America's hunger for the written word has remained strong over the last century, book publication and sales practices have changed dramatically.

THE BEGINNING

Johann Gutenberg invented a printing press with movable type in the 15th century, making mechanical production of books possible for the first time. Gutenberg's printing press provided welcome relief from copying texts by hand, and by the early 16th century, France, England, Spain, Italy, and the Netherlands all had small printing industries.

The first book printed in America was the 1639 *Bay Psalm Book* by the Cambridge Press. Puritans in the Massachusetts Bay Colony established the press as an aid to their missionary efforts; they

Communication

published religious books and hymnals to be used in converting their Native American neighbors. The Cambridge Press had moved to Boston by 1700, making that city a major publishing center — a distinction Boston retains today. By 1763, all of the 13 original colonies were operating at least one printing plant, making Bibles and almanacs — the two best-selling types of books during the early colonial years — readily available.

By the end of the 1700s, however, literary works were outselling religious and how-to offerings. This diversification of book readership laid the groundwork for the publishing business as we know it today.

THE EARLY CONTRIBUTORS

The first American publisher whose business resembled the modern publishing house was Mathew Carey, who as a young man had worked for Benjamin Franklin in Paris. An Irish immigrant, Carey arrived in Philadelphia in 1784 and started publishing almost immediately. He began with a newspaper and two magazines, then turned his attention to books. His publishing house, which came to be known as M. Carey & Son, was one of the few major publishing houses to operate in a large American city by the beginning of the Civil War.

Like Carey's company, many of these early publishing houses were controlled by their founding families. Joining M. Carey & Son in Philadelphia was J. B. Lippincott & Company. In Boston, Charles C. Little and James Brown created Little, Brown & Company. Henry Oscar Houghton, the preeminent publishing figure in New England, entered into a partnership with George Harrison Mifflin to form Houghton Mifflin & Company in New York. The Harper brothers, John and James, founded Harper's, which published Herman Melville's *Moby-Dick* in 1851; by the mid-19th century, Harper's was the largest publishing house in America.

Many of these early publishing companies are still thriving today; they often ensured their survival by specializing in a particular type of book. D. Appleton & Company, for instance, publisher of *Alice in Wonderland* and Darwin's *Origin of Species*, did a brisk business in educational textbooks and was among the first publishers to offer Spanish-language texts in America. A. S. Barnes & Company was the first publishing house dedicated exclusively to educational books. Others, however, did not follow the path of specialization. Charles Scribner's company published religious texts and popular fiction alike. E. P. Dutton & Company started out as a specialist in religious works but eventually branched out into general trade publishing.

Two legends in the world of New York publishing, Henry Holt and Frank Nelson Doubleday, exemplify two very different approaches to the business. Holt was born in Baltimore and educated at Yale University and Columbia Law School. A would-be writer who sought financial stability, he never practiced law but worked in publishing instead. In 1873 he established Henry Holt & Company, becoming a major player by 1880. Holt, with his own writerly aspirations, exemplifies the publisher as purveyor of literary art and cultural knowledge.

Frank Nelson Doubleday, on the other hand, viewed publishing not as a staid literary endeavor, but as a business. Doubleday started as an apprentice to Charles Scribner, and his first major coup was his acquisition of all of Rudyard Kipling's stories from three different publishers. He reissued them in one complete, corrected volume, which he newly prefaced and entitled the *Outward Bound Edition*. It sold many thousands of copies. But tensions between Scribner and Doubleday forced the shrewd apprentice to leave. After a three-year partnership with magazine publisher S. S. McClure, Doubleday allied himself with former *Atlantic* editor Walter Hines Page to form Doubleday, Page & Company in 1900. Doubleday's contributions to the publishing industry included improvements upon the fledgling practice of selling by mail, and opening a chain of bookstores as a "selling laboratory." His innovations of nearly a century ago are standard practices today.

Charles C. Little, cofounder (with James Brown) of Little, Brown & Company. His publishing house, established in 1837, still operates under the same name today.

GENERAL BUSINESS PRACTICES

John Farrar characterized the history of book publishing as the story of a business "attended by feuds and contradictions. . . . The miracle has been that publishing developed at all, so often has it been in the hands of the sharp and downright (sometimes magnificently) pigheaded individualist." Often, because publishers were so opinionated about what they considered worthy of printing, they would reject a literary manuscript only to see it accepted and published by another company to great commercial and critical success. Even though publishers made numerous miscalculations—and capitalized on those made by competitors—they took their role as brokers of information in a free society quite seriously. While their judgments of literary manuscripts were often clouded by their personal tastes, book publishers didn't usually let their political views stand in the way of their duty to dispense objective information.

Though Wall Street disdained the publishing world's naivete in not making financial gain its first priority, most publishers did maintain a healthy bottom line. Nearly 200 of the firms founded before 1900 survived beyond the turn of the century, and by the 1950s, almost one-third remained under the control of their founding families. Improved methods of communication and transportation enabled large publishing houses in major cities to sell books nationwide in the years following the Civil War. As a result, the big companies grew bigger. Intercontinental transactions took place as English publishing houses like Oxford University Press and Macmillan, Longmans, Green, & Company set up offices in New York City; American publishers like Putnam, Harper's, Appleton, and Lippincott did the same in London. The British companies intended to publish new works in America, whereas the Americans only wanted to purchase British titles and reprint them in the United States.

Publisher Frank Nelson Doubleday. Among his contributions to the book business is the opening of a "selling laboratory"—an early book-store chain.

By 1870, New York was the capital of book publication. A decade later, Chicago, which had been an important book distribution center before the Civil War, became a secondary hub. Indianapolis, Minneapolis, Cleveland, Cincinnati, and San Francisco also played significant roles. Boston's prominence was buttressed by publishing houses in nearby Hartford, Springfield, and Andover.

By this time, the modern process of evaluating manuscripts was in use. Editorial assistants skimmed the "slush pile"—the hundreds of manuscripts that poured in to major publishers. When publishers could no longer read each manuscript themselves they hired readers to do this time-consuming job for about five dollars per book.

Some publishers also began to generate their own ideas for books, then farm them out to writers. These "literary factories," modeled after operations in Berlin, flourished briefly in the United States during the 1890s. Their mostly female staff would scan newspapers for sensational stories, then submit them to male managers, who in turn selected the items that would be assigned to writers.

Although American readers had a bigger appetite for fiction, nonfiction became an increasingly popular category. Publishers responded by inventing the nonfiction series, collected volumes such as Lippincott's Reason Why books, which originated in 1869. Putnam released numerous nonfiction series, among them the 10-volume *Campaigns of the Civil War*. It became a common practice to enlist prominent university professors or other experts to develop or oversee these projects. Publishers also scanned periodicals for subject matter, often haphazardly compiling and publishing anthologies to meet the new demand for encyclopedic information books.

This view down one of its streets shows just how important books had become to the life of New York City by the late 1800s. The tall buildings to the far right house publishers of encyclopedias, dictionaries, and literary supplements. The Astor Library (the shorter building in the center of the picture) stands just next door.

But publishers didn't want to be perceived as crass businessmen, so they also tried to continue releasing "good literature." Many publishers postured as unselfish and underpaid, reveling all the while in their positions as the captains of "the worst business in the world." In 1905, Walter Hines Page wrote in his *Publisher's Confession* that publishing was akin to teaching or preaching. "A good book is a Big Thing, a thing to be thankful to heaven for," he pontificated.

In reality, however, good books were few and far between. Mediocre writing outnumbered first-rate manuscripts at a staggering rate. The pressure to produce quality books prompted most publishers to engage in unsavory trade practices such as international piracy. Still, the industry had lower financial stakes than most other fields, so it is fair to say that many publishers thrived on the simple excitement of literature itself—and on their privileged positions as the judges of what constituted good writing. As they do today, successful publishers made their fortunes by producing best-sellers and by maintaining a backlist of perennially requested works.

The desire for a wide readership also spurred many book publishers of the time to acquire subsidiary magazines. Inspired by the success of *Harper's Monthly* and *Harper's Weekly*, Boston publisher Ticknor & Fields purchased *The Atlantic Monthly* in 1859. After 1865, many major publishing houses had their own magazines, among them *Scribner's Monthly*, *Lippincott's Magazine*, and *Harper's Bazar* (changed in 1929 to *Harper's Bazaar*). Publishers shrewdly used their periodicals to advertise their books and to print serialized versions of novels, which helped hardcover book sales. These literary magazines could not compete with the flood of new, general-interest magazines, though. Publications such as *Ladies' Home Journal*, *The Saturday Evening Post*, and *Cosmopolitan* devoted some of their pages to popular fiction, but they also explored other topics. Only a few book publishers' magazines survived beyond the First World War.

One lasting innovation in the publishing business was not a new product, but a new job. Henry Holt, who refused to give authors written contracts, once declared, "Royalties exceeding ten percent are immoral." Publishers like Holt created a need for literary agents, who negotiated on behalf of writers for better financial terms and increased creative control.

Like the job description for literary agents, the production pattern for conventional hardcover books remains today much as it was during the last century. Publishing had two seasons, spring and fall. Stores were fully stocked with new fall publications by October to allow ample shopping time before the holidays.

SALES TECHNIQUES

The method of bookselling in post–Civil War America, on the other hand, was a far cry from the multilevel, cappuccino-serving bookstores we browse today. In the early 1900s, there was approximately one bookstore for every 28,000 Americans. Ninety percent of all books were sold by door-to-door sales agents who usually covered large rural territories.

The practice of soliciting individual orders for books was not new, and many distinguished Americans worked as book agents at some point in their lives. While George Washington was a surveyor in Virginia, he supplemented his income by selling Bydell's *The London of Stoke-on-Trent Square*. Another future president, Rutherford B. Hayes, sold Baxter's *Lives of the Saints* to earn money as a boy growing up in Ohio. And such famous writers as Mark Twain, Henry Wadsworth Longfellow, and Daniel Webster sold books door-to-door early in their careers.

The New York Library was founded in 1895 and opened in 1911. The expansion and development of public library systems around the turn of the century made a wealth of information available to citizens of all economic levels.

Books were often released in overpriced hardback volumes designed for an unsophisticated rural public. At the lower-priced end of the continuum were self-help books, etiquette guides, tales of the Wild West, and even mild pornography. At the higher-priced end were art books, encyclopedias, dictionaries, cookbooks, nonfiction science and history books, and multivolume sets of fiction.

Subscription book agents charged up to four times retail bookstore prices. Sometimes they engaged in unethical business practices, such as telling customers that extra profit from overpriced volumes would benefit some imaginary charity. Disabled Civil War veterans were particularly adept at milking the sympathies and pocketbooks of their teary-eyed customers by telling them true or invented war stories. In 1901, traveling book agents could make as much as $12,000 a year. By 1905, publishers also used direct-mail sales brochures to attract customers.

As it became easier for Americans everywhere to purchase books, publishers looked for ways of attracting this growing market. Advertising began in earnest in the late 1800s. The art of writing ad copy for books evolved slowly: one briefly employed copywriter described Walt Whitman's *Leaves of Grass* as "a daisy—and don't you forget it." Some publishers hired men to walk the streets wearing "sandwich boards" advertising their latest offering. Funk and Wagnalls advertised its Standard Dictionary by hanging posters in streetcars. Advertising copy was hyperbolic, touting every new novel as "the best since *A Tale of Two Cities*" and every new writer as "the next Dickens." Publishers spent huge sums advertising their books. By 1900, the industry was allocating $5 million a year for that purpose alone.

REPRINTS

As their marketing and advertising expenditures soared, publishers tried to contain the cost of book production. In the 1870s the popularity of inexpensive paperbacks and cheap hardcover books skyrocketed. These mass market materials first appeared in the 1840s, when publishers realized that most English and French novels were not protected under American copyright laws, and when the industry developed a cheap grade of groundwood paper on which to print these pirated books.

The second proliferation of these paperbacks might have been induced by competition from a newspaper. In 1873, the *New York Tribune* began selling inexpensive "Tribune Novels." By 1875, publishing houses had responded by selling cheap reprints of books that had already sold well in hardcover. No-frills reprint houses liked to call themselves "libraries," as in The Lakeside Library, George Munro's Seaside Library, or the Fireside Library. They "borrowed" existing works from authors without paying royalties. This unethical practice saved publishers money.

Pirating books to save money was nothing new; Harper's had long since released its hardcover Family Library and Library of Select Novels, which consisted almost entirely of stolen British works. The reprints appearing in the 1870s took cost cutting a step further, however. Publishers scrimped on production costs by making books in the relatively small quarto size (about 10 by 12 inches) and by cramming up to three columns of narrowly spaced type onto each page. Most reprinted books were paper-covered or issued without any covers. They sold for 10 to 20 cents each, and they were extremely popular with American consumers.

By 1877, 2.5 million cheap reprints had been published—a number large enough to hurt sales of conventional hardcovers. Some conventional publishers couldn't resist cashing in on the brisk reprint business; Harper's Franklin Square Library was established to reissue the publishing giant's own reprints at greatly reduced prices.

In 1882, reprint houses went one step further by issuing books in a still smaller duodecimal size (about 5 by 8 inches), which customers eagerly bought. The publishers' quest for thrift was further aided by the U.S. Postal Service in 1885, when sending rates were cut in half. By 1886, virtually every major publisher had its own cheap reprint line. Fully one-third of the 4,500 titles released that year were inexpensive, mass market editions.

American readers benefited from the publishing industry's efforts to cut costs because they could buy great works of literature at rock-bottom prices. But this wave of reprinting was curtailed with the passing of international copyright laws in 1891. Reprint houses reluctantly turned to American authors—to whom they had to pay royalties. To help make up for the resulting losses, publishers employed unusual distribution and promotion methods. One of the strangest was the paperback vending machine. Reprint houses also made deals with soap manufacturers, who included the books as free gifts with every soap purchase. An estimated 2 million paperbacks were given away in soap promotions at the turn of the century.

AMERICAN READING TASTES

In the years after the colonial period, fiction had consistently outsold other types of reading material. Between 1890 and 1910, Americans seemed to have a particularly unquenchable thirst for novels.

Female novelists were especially successful during the late 19th century. In fact, the first millionaire fiction writer in America made her fortune writing family novels—a genre dominated by women. Gene Stratton-Porter had sold 9 million copies of her 19 "Home and Jesus" books by the end of her career in the early 1900s. She netted about $2 million in the process.

Paperbound dime novels were exceptionally popular at the turn of the century. The publishing house of Street & Smith, founded in 1889, issued a series of Westerns and detective stories that became so popular that their original authors were overwhelmed by reader demand. Street & Smith hired ghostwriters to churn out new titles at the rate of one per week. Similarly, Frederic Day's famous Nick Carter series was farmed out to five writers, and 18 of the works credited to Horatio Alger, Jr., were actually ghostwritten after his death!

One of Street & Smith's most prolific hacks was William Gilbert Patten. Under the pen name of Burt L. Standish, he created the Frank Merriwell series, which chronicled the adventures of a solidly all-American boy. Street & Smith would eventually publish over 200 Frank Merriwell books—all dictated by Patten to a team of secretaries. Street & Smith's book factory catered to the reading tastes of the time. One series promoted patriotic ideals; another, the Diamond Handbooks, instructed readers in everything from letter writing to dream interpretation. The formula proved successful; by the turn of the century, Street & Smith was one of the world's largest publishers.

Groups of books with common themes, such as the industrialization of society, fantasy, adventure, and rural American life often took turns on the best-seller list. Early best-sellers included novels holding appeal for children and adults alike, such as Anna Sewell's *Black Beauty*, which had sold 3 million copies by 1909. Beginning in 1894, "high romance" novels set in the historic past enjoyed a long reign of popularity.

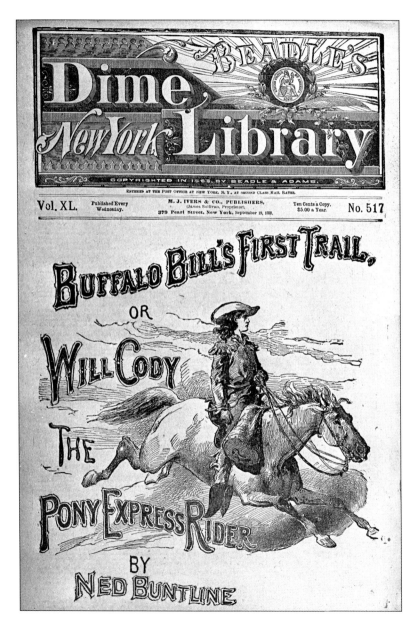

Paperbound dime novels were immensely popular in the late 19th and early 20th centuries. The book pictured here deals with a favorite theme — the Wild West. The following these books gained among young men, as well as the huge readership of romance novels among women, prompted one critic of the time to sniff that readers were being "novelized into absolute idiocy."

Reviewers typically saw these popular publications as mediocre at best. Although many best-selling books had moral themes, critics attacked novels for either their sensationalism or their disturbing realism in depicting social issues. Critics denounced novels as "the opiate of the masses," just as critics denigrate television today. One magazine declared, "Millions of young girls and hundreds of thousands of young men are novelized into absolute idiocy. Novel-readers are like opium-smokers: the more they have of it, the more they want of it."

Critics blamed publishers for cynically pandering to public tastes. Publishers claimed they were merely supplying what the people wanted. But even during the height of America's love affair with the novel, there were detractors who claimed—as they still do now—that the novel was a dying art form. In 1902, Jules Verne said, "I do not think there will be any novels or romances in fifty or a hundred years from now. . . ."

Fortunately for the book lovers of today, Jules Verne was wrong.

Newspapers

SINCE THE COLONIAL ERA, NEWSPAPERS HAVE PLAYED A vital role in disseminating information to the American people. During the 1800s, the newspaper business underwent dramatic changes as readership expanded and editors and publishers transformed editorial content.

THE BEGINNING

The first American newspaper, printed in Boston in 1690 by John Harris, was entitled *Publick Occurrenses Both Forreign and Domestick*. By 1750, 14 weekly newspapers were being published in six American colonies. Newspapers were a medium of both patriot and Loyalist views during the Revolution, and often their content amounted to propaganda. The newspaper was overshadowed by books and magazines in the first half of the 19th century but gained many faithful readers—despite the popularity of novels—from 1850 to 1900.

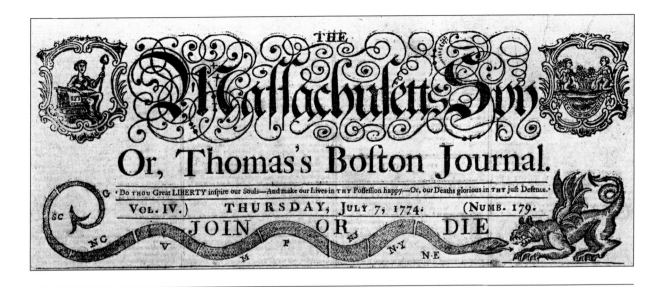

Masthead of the *Massachusetts Sun*, a colonial newspaper. The slogan, "Join or die," makes this publisher's patriotic leaning clear on the eve of the Revolutionary War.

Several economic factors assisted this upsurge of newspaper readership in the late 1800s. As urban populations grew, so did the number of businesses to serve them. People needed the news in print; businesses needed a forum in which to advertise. Newspapers were the ideal answer to both needs. Increased circulation meant more advertising revenue, so competition became keen as each newspaper strived to reach the largest readership possible.

NEWSPAPERS AND THE RECONSTRUCTION PERIOD

Newspaper publishers were no less opinionated about editorial content than their counterparts in the book business, but during the years following the Civil War, they began to look beyond local events or their personal circumstances in an attempt to stimulate thoughtful discussion among their readers. This trend was most noticeable in the South, where newspapers tried to offer southern readers moral and philosophical guidance.

Henry W. Grady was one journalist who tried to provide a sense of direction to the war-torn South. Son of a wealthy and influential Georgia family, Grady wrote for the *Atlanta Constitution* as a law student, then assumed the editorship of the *Courier* in Rome, Georgia, after graduation. He quickly discovered that the town's press and politics were incredibly corrupt—and that Rome's citizens seemed to like this state of affairs. Hopeful that things would be different in a larger city, Grady established the *Herald* in Atlanta, but was soon disappointed. He finally took a job with the *New York Herald* as its Atlanta correspondent.

Grady finally had a national forum for his views. His articles and editorials urged the South to break with its traditionally agrarian way of life and industrialize. But it was his suggestion that blacks and whites should live as equals that got Grady the most attention. He received criticism and hate mail from some southern readers, but northern newspaper publishers embraced his ideals and reprinted his editorials. In 1879, he purchased one-fourth of the *Atlanta Constitution*, and by 1886, he was a frequent public speaker on such topics as "The Race Problem in the South." After Grady's death in 1889, the *Constitution* carried on his crusade to convert the old Confederacy.

Another unconventional thinker of the day, Henry Watterson, had even more liberal views on race relations in the new South. During his 50-year career as editor of the *Louisville Courier-Journal*, his articles suggested that the South protect the rights of its emancipated slaves in order to get back some of the rights it had lost to the North in the war.

He also used his pen to support political candidates who shared his views. When one of these, Samuel J. Tilden, apparently won the presidency in 1876 only to have his election disputed and eventually overturned under questionable circumstances, the editor gave up mixing journalism and party politics. Watterson continued promoting his own vision of post–Civil War America, however. At the end of his long career, he won a 1917 Pulitzer Prize for his editorials on World War I.

MUCKRAKING

While journalists in the South attempted to stir the public conscience, newspapers in the wide-open West (U.S. territory from Ohio to the Pacific) capitalized on the public's delight in raw sensationalism. In Chicago, Wilbur F. Storey's *Times* indulged readers with titillating tales of sex, crime, and public hangings. *Times* headlines were typically alliterated, as in "Death's Debauch," "Frail Females," and "Feet First." Shortly before his death in 1884, Storey was judged insane.

In Denver, Frederick Gilmer Bonfils and Harry Heye Tammen—two men with little knowledge of journalism but plenty of insight into human nature—turned their meeting at a bar into a highly profitable newspaper. Bonfils was a Missourian with a background that was as shady as it was varied: having been thrown out of West Point Military Academy before becoming involved in fraudulent real estate deals, he used his considerable sales talent to run an illegal lottery in Kansas City. When he was exposed by the *Star*, a Kansas City newspaper dedicated to stamping out corruption, Bonfils fled to Denver. There he met Tammen, a former bowling pin setter from Baltimore, who tended bar at the Windsor Hotel. Tammen convinced his new friend to invest $12,500 in the faltering *Denver Evening Post*. In October of 1895, Bonfils and Tammen unveiled the new paper, shortening its name to *The Post*.

Henry Watterson, longtime editor of the *Louisville Courier-Journal*, was one of the Reconstruction's most liberal thinkers, urging southern states to safeguard the rights of emancipated slaves.

The Post proclaimed itself "The Paper With a Heart and Soul," and its motto was "So the People May Know." The paper's philosophy, that "a dog fight in a Denver street is more important than a war in Europe," was immediately evident. With screaming headlines in large, red type, *The Post* proceeded to libel public officials and ferret out supposed criminals under the guise of working for the public good. The practice of searching for real or imagined misconduct on the part of public figures, known as muckraking, helped *The Post* increase its circulation from 4,000 to 83,000. Its readers outnumbered those of the other three Denver papers combined.

In San Francisco, the journalistic climate was even hotter. *The Chronicle* dominated the newspaper business for 25 years after the Civil War. Founded in 1865 by brothers Charles and Michael H. De Young, this newspaper was zealous in its commitment to community service. But fighting an unscrupulous politician got Charles De Young into trouble. He shot and wounded a corrupt mayoral candidate, whose son, in revenge, shot and killed him in 1880. The surviving brother, Michael H. De Young, turned *The Chronicle* from crime-fighting crusader into a mouthpiece for Republican conservatism.

SERVING THE PUBLIC

Although muckraking journalism became an increasingly prevalent method of boosting newspaper sales in the late 19th century, many journalists during this period refrained from lurid sensationalism as they exposed corruption.

continued on page 53

A cloud of dust in his wake, a Pony Express rider races toward his destination. Riders faced blistering heat, blinding snow, and the occasional wild animal attack along a punishing route that took them from Missouri to California.

This lithograph of a railway mail car in the early 1900s shows the volume of mail that postal workers had to contend with as they sorted letters in transit.

No. 599
OCT. 5, 1907 — FRANK MERRIWELL'S WORST BOY — FIVE CENTS

TIP TOP WEEKLY

An Ideal Publication for the American Youth

Dime novel hero Frank Merriwell (in front of canoe) braves the rapids. Burt L. Standish (whose real name was William Gilbert Patten) created the valiant, upstanding Frank Merriwell character and by the early 1900s had written him into over 200 adventures for publishing giant Street & Smith.

As the urban population increased at the turn of the century, city newspapers relied on eye-catching advertisements to attract readers. This poster for the *New York Sunday World* gets its message across with the colorful sweep of a lady's skirt and the promise of fun.

continued from page 48

Still others in the newspaper business used their publications as forums for their personal opinions. Joseph Medill, for example, who served as editor-in-chief of the *Chicago Tribune* from 1863 to 1899, said that a newspaper should not be "the organ of one man, however high, no clique or ring, however influential, no faction, however fanatical or demonstrative," and that newspapers should always "follow the line of common sense." But Medill's level-headed statement belied the reality that his *Tribune* was strongly flavored with his personal convictions. Sometimes, his opinions were uplifting: the *Tribune*'s famous editorial after fire devastated the city in 1871 urged, "Cheer up! Chicago shall rise again!" The piece boosted Chicago's collective morale and ensured Medill's mayoral victory the following year.

Back in the editor's chair in 1874, however, Medill used his paper to promulgate his extreme—and sometimes disturbing—views. "The simplest plan . . ." he wrote in an editorial about unemployed people, "is to [put] arsenic in the supplies of food furnished to the unemployed or the tramp. This produces death in a short time and is a warning to other tramps to keep out of the neighborhood."

One shining example of an editor who lived up to his ideal of public service was William Rockhill Nelson, founder and editor of the *Kansas City Evening Star*. For Nelson, "community service" meant that the *Star* would be local, "a family newspaper for Kansas City families."

He believed that reporters were the most valuable people on a newspaper staff; Nelson's reporters were sent out to investigate every corner of Kansas City, a place then rife with corruption and violence. Under Nelson's editorship, the *Star* exposed rigged elections, gambling rings, and the poor upkeep of the city's streets. As a result, corruption in Kansas City was brought under control, and the *Star* prospered through the close of the century.

After the California gold rush of the 1840s, newspaper publishers headed west, too. This newspaper staff poses in front of its "office." By the late 1800s, prospectors got the lowdown on happenings in mining towns as well as national news from the *Daily Reporter* and numerous small papers like it.

STAMPING OUT WIRE SERVICE FRAUD

Like Nelson, Victor Fremont Lawson was concerned with maintaining the integrity of the newspaper business. In 1876, he bought Chicago's *Daily News* from its founder, Melville Stone. Retaining Stone as editor-in-chief, Lawson strived to publish an honest, thorough, and affordable newspaper. His efforts in Chicago would ultimately have less of an impact than Nelson's had in Kansas City, but Victor Fremont Lawson would be instrumental in reforming the nation's wire services.

Wire services were telegraph lines—an emerging technology in the late 19th century—that provided stories to newspapers. There were two wire service agencies at the time: the United Press (UP), an outside business that sold news items for a fee; and the Associated Press (AP), a cooperative enterprise made up of elected people in the newspaper business who shared the cost of collecting and distributing news. Around 1890, Lawson and members of AP's western division began to suspect that the New York division of AP was involved in rigging financial wire reports to benefit New York businesses, giving them an unfair advantage over businesses in the rest of the country. Lawson also noticed that many UP reports were identical to AP stories.

AP's western division appointed Lawson and two others to an investigative team. Within a year, Lawson had discovered that the three principle owners of UP were controlling the content of AP stories as part of a secret deal they made with five prominent AP members. Through this illegal deal, UP received AP's news for free and the money UP saved lined the five AP traitors' pockets.

After the scandal was exposed, UP filed for bankruptcy. Lawson served as president of AP from 1894 to 1900. Newspaper publishers who didn't join AP formed a new wire service called the Publishers' Press, known today as United Press International (UPI).

LEGENDS OF NEWSPAPER PUBLISHING

Two of the most influential newspaper publishers of the 19th century were Joseph Pulitzer and William Randolph Hearst. The upstart Hearst and the seasoned Pulitzer would eventually run dueling publications In New York City. They would push each other beyond the limits of conventional journalism—resulting in both inspired reporting and blatant muckraking.

Joseph Pulitzer, a Hungarian immigrant, had worked his way up from obscurity to become a successful publisher and politician in St. Louis before he purchased the *New York World* in 1883. Pulitzer soon transformed the penny religious daily into a steamy hotbed of sex, scandal, and corruption, outselling competitors like the *New York Herald*. The *World* became America's largest daily, employing 1,300 people with an annual budget of $2 million. But when Hearst blew into town in 1896, Pulitzer found himself reaching for a new standard yet again.

The newspaper business was in William Randolph Hearst's blood. His father, George Hearst, had resuscitated San Francisco's failing *Evening Examiner*. By 1887, it was California's most successful paper, boasting 20,000 regular readers. When the elder Hearst handed over the reigns to his son, William Randolph, the *Examiner* adopted the sensationalist tone of Pulitzer's *New York World*.

The junior Hearst replaced longtime editor Clarence Greathouse with Arthur McEwen, who would later coin the term "gee whiz" news. The expression derived from McEwen's reaction upon viewing the *Examiner's* inflammatory headlines. "Gee whiz" journalism catapulted the *Examiner* to new heights with a circulation of 60,000 in 1893.

Hearst turned sensationalism into an art form and added the extra dimension of photography to his paper. He hired the most intrepid writers he could find, reporters like Petey Bigelow, who once pursued a

Joseph Medill, who managed the *Chicago Tribune* from 1863 to 1899 (with one three-year absence from the editor's chair to serve as the city's mayor). Medill wrote commentaries that were at times offensive and boorish, but he was smart enough to confine his views to the *Tribune's* editorial page.

Before publishers like William Randolph Hearst enhanced their newspapers with photographs, the quality of a paper's illustrations could determine its success or failure. This front page of *Frank Leslie's Illustrated Newspaper* demonstrates why Leslie became known as the father of pictorial journalism.

pair of train robbers to their mountain hideout just to interview them. Politically, Hearst painted the *Examiner* as a protector of the people, allied to no one but the honest taxpayer. He was also an ingenious promoter who organized stunts like flying over San Francisco in a hot-air balloon, then sending a flock of homing pigeons back to his offices with descriptions and photos of the city's skyline.

When Hearst moved to New York in 1896 to start a new paper called the *Journal*, Pulitzer's position as the journalistic king of New York was seriously threatened. The *Journal*'s staff materialized in typical Hearst fashion; he hired many talented writers away from Pulitzer's *World* and other publications. He was responsible for introducing comic strips to newspapers. One comic, Richard Outcault's "Yellow Kid," would lend its name to the intensely sensational type of reporting—"yellow journalism"—that developed in the final years of the 19th century. From the *Journal*'s editorial pages came distinctly working-class appeals for eight-hour workdays, labor rights, and women's suffrage. All of these elements helped ensure the *Journal*'s popularity with the masses, although Hearst may have taken things too far.

Hearst has been blamed with starting the Spanish-American War in his efforts to outsell the *World*. In 1895, the small island nation of Cuba revolted against Spanish control after losing the Ten Years' War (1868–78) to Spain. American public sympathy rested with the Cuban patriots, but the United States initially refrained from becoming involved. But when one of Hearst's Cuban correspondents requested permission to return to the States, Hearst wired back, "Please remain," promising, "You furnish the pictures and I'll furnish the war."

A tidal wave of warmongering followed—in both the *Journal* and the *World*—which consisted of editorials, photos, and headlines that

Hungarian immigrant Joseph Pulitzer became an American success story. The publisher, a shrewd judge of popular tastes, transformed the *World* from a penny religious paper into a crusading, eye-grabbing daily that outsold every other in the nation. The prestigious Pulitzer Prize—still awarded annually—is funded by his considerable estate.

promoted the cause of war with frenzied urgency. Most of the stories were sensationalized accounts of Spanish atrocities against the Cuban rebels. The circulations of both papers soon shot past one million.

Hearst's and Pulitzer's papers not only created a favorable climate for American involvement in the conflict; their sensational reporting was probably also largely responsible for President William McKinley's

decision to send American troops to Cuba in April of 1898. On the night of February 15, the U.S.S. *Maine* had sunk after an explosion in Havana Harbor. Two hundred and sixty American servicemen were killed. Although its cause was never determined, the *Journal*, the *World*, and many other American papers immediately attributed the sinking to a Spanish bomb.

Edwin Lawrence Godkin, editor of the influential *New York Post*, bitterly censured the "gross misrepresentation of facts" appearing in the *Journal* and the *World*. In the *Post*, Godkin fumed: "Nothing so disgraceful as the behavior of two of these newspapers this week has been known in the history of American Journalism. . . . It is a crying shame that men should work such mischief simply in order to sell more papers."

Hearst and Pulitzer, who spared no expense to cover the war, both suffered financially. But Pulitzer also suffered in health, and in the decade before his death in 1911, he relinquished his working-class readership to Hearst. Pulitzer's sensationalist *World* was reincarnated as a forum for liberal ideas until it went out of business in 1931. Hearst went on to prosper in the newspaper business—as well as in the magazine and real estate businesses. But many New York readers, weary of the shrill headlines of muckraking and yellow journalism, turned to the *Times*, which promised them "All the news that's fit to print."

Magazines

IT MAY BE HARD TO BELIEVE NOW, WHEN THERE EXISTS A magazine for every interest and every budget, but periodicals were once considered luxury items. The American magazine industry had to meet several challenges to become the viable industry that it is today. Among them were competition from newspapers and books, a potential audience with diverse interests, and an early lack of visual appeal.

THE BEGINNING

The first American magazine was published in Philadelphia on February 16, 1741, by Andrew Bradford. Entitled *American Magazine, or a Monthly View of the Political State of the British Colonies*, it appeared just three days before Benjamin Franklin's *General Magazine, and Historical Chronicle, for All the British Plantations in America*. Before these two offerings, if wealthy colonists wanted to read magazines, they imported them from England. Early American periodicals were imitations of English magazines; it was not until 1779, when H. E. Brackenridge published his *United States Magazine*, that the medium assumed a distinctly American character.

American cities teemed with newsboys at the turn of the century, so selling magazines was a logical extension of this sidewalk enterprise. *The Saturday Evening Post*, shown in this promotion, was one magazine that competed successfully against newspapers.

To Any Boy
who answers this advertisement

The Saturday Evening Post
OF PHILADELPHIA

Will send *entirely without charge* 10 copies of next week's issue of the magazine, to be sold at Five Cents each.

The **Fifty Cents** thus earned will provide capital with which to start business, after which a supply will be sent each week at the special wholesale price. Any boy with the average amount of enterprise and push can earn money each week in leisure hours and be independent.

In Addition
to the profits earned, $250.00 in money will be divided among those boys who in **August** increase their average weekly sale to fifteen copies.

If you want a share
and will try the plan, send a postal and you will receive next week's supply of 10 copies, with full instructions, and a dainty little booklet containing photographs of some of our most successful boys, and letters from them telling in their own way how they did it.

Circulation Bureau
The Curtis Publishing Company, Philadelphia, Pa.

Eighteenth-century magazines covered topics such as fashion, society, religion, politics, and etiquette, interspersed with news and short stories. There were few magazines in circulation until the early 19th century. In 1825, the approximately 100 magazines in print had begun to specialize; periodicals about specific interests such as agriculture, medicine, and theater appeared.

After 1825, the number of magazines increased, in part because of the invention of the cylinder press—the first major advancement in printing since movable type. By 1850, about 600 magazines were available in America. The industry had begun to adopt some of its present-day characteristics: illustrations began to accompany text, and publishers, who had rarely paid writers before, started trying to attract talent. Thus, paid magazine writers began to tailor their articles to specific publications. These developments paved the way for magazines to continue multiplying in number and type through the remainder of the 1800s.

COMPETITION FROM OTHER PRINT MEDIA

Magazines sold for about 35 cents per copy, which was much more than the cost of a newspaper. This made them prohibitively expensive for many Americans. By the late 1880s, however, magazine publishers realized that they had to increase circulation to be competitive with newspapers. *Lippincott's* led the trend by reducing its price to 20 cents; other magazines followed suit until many of them had dropped to a nickel per issue. However, newspaper publishers still dismissed the magazine as a "newspaper in a dress suit."

Many well-known magazines, such as the *Atlantic*, the *Century*, and *Scribner's,* stole some editorial thunder from newspapers by imitating and expanding upon their content. Periodicals that had previously emphasized literature now discussed social problems like urban housing conditions, the rising number of divorces, homeless children, and race relations. Magazines also explored issues such as foreign trade and international diplomacy, and politicians, including Grover Cleveland and Theodore Roosevelt, became frequent contributors.

Magazines competed with books as well. In response to the novel craze at the turn of the century, general-interest magazines devoted as much as a third of their editorial space to serialized works of fiction. Periodical fiction anthologies were consistently popular. *Short Stories*, founded in 1896, lasted until the 1950s. Another short-story magazine, *Red Book* (known today as the popular women's periodical *Redbook*), added a photographic supplement to its pages and saw circulation shoot to 300,000 a mere two years after its inception in 1903.

THE USE OF PHOTOGRAPHY

Red Book wasn't the only magazine that prospered with the addition of photographs. Photography had existed since 1842, but it wasn't until the latter part of the century, after the cost of producing photographic plates decreased, that magazines could afford to include photos. In 1884 the *Century* became the first magazine to print halftone photographic images. Within a decade halftone photographs were commonplace, with some magazines—*Cosmopolitan*, for instance—relying on them for almost all of their illustrations.

SPECIAL-INTEREST MAGAZINES

As it was with book publication, New York City was the capital of the magazine business by 1880. Boston, home of the popular children's magazine *Youth's Companion*, was a close second, followed by Philadelphia and Chicago.

Improved lithographic and photographic reproduction techniques meant that magazine covers themselves became works of art after the 1870s. Beautiful cover art, such as the horse-drawn sleigh on this issue of *Harper's*, graced art journals and general-interest magazines alike.

Wherever magazines were being published, they were diversifying and specializing at a rapid rate in the late 1800s. The Centennial Exposition of 1876, which exhibited American inventions such as the phonograph and the telephone, helped to stimulate the creation of

continued on page 73

Communication

Life magazine—which flourishes today as a general-interest publication—was founded by Harvard graduates who saw a need for satire that would appeal to learned readers. The cover of this issue scathingly mocks U.S. involvement in the Spanish-American War.

OUR EXPANSIVE UNCLE.
BUT IT'S ONLY TEMPORARY.

This cartoon, from the satire magazine *Puck*, addresses the issue of sensational, inaccurate journalism — among other evils of the newspaper business. In the late 19th century, rivalries between magazines and dailies sometimes turned bitter.

The *Saturday Evening Post* steadfastly continued printing lithographs long after photographic reproduction became feasible. This 1916 Norman Rockwell illustration of an unlucky boy and his mischievous tormentors is characteristic of the *Post* covers that made him famous.

THE SATURDAY EVENING POST

An Ill____ted Weekly
Founded A____ __8 *by* Benj. Franklin

MAY 20, 1916   5c. THE COPY

Norman
Rockwell

Suggestions for
The Hostess

VOGUE

July 15th 1916
Price 25 Cents

The Vogue Company
CONDÉ NAST, Publisher

The lighthearted and colorful cover art of this 1916 issue of *Vogue* magazine instantly sets it apart from earlier publications devoted to promoting women's rights. Founded in 1892 by editor Josephine Redding, *Vogue* was a repository of fashion and beauty tips.

71

In this Currier and Ives lithograph, entitled "The Progress of the Century," the emblems of progress all relate to communication. Improved transportation over land and sea, telegraphy, and high-speed printing presses all enlarged the world of the individual, while at the same time fostering a sense of connectedness between the American people.

continued from page 67

scientific magazines. *Scientific American* was one of several general science magazines that were in circulation by 1885 to satisfy America's growing curiosity about emerging technologies.

National Geographic was perhaps the most prominent science magazine of the time. Founded in 1888 by a wealthy lawyer named Gardiner Greene Hubbard, the magazine was first issued only to the 1,400 members of the National Geographic Society. In addition to funding from Hubbard, who was interested in exploring Alaska, *National Geographic* also received support from Hubbard's son-in-law, Alexander Graham Bell. In 1903, Gilbert Grosvenor took over as editor, transforming it into a popular magazine to which anyone could subscribe. He made sure that *National Geographic* was lavishly illustrated with maps and photographs and full of fascinating eyewitness accounts of the world and its wonders. Grosvenor's factual and entertaining formula has changed little to this day, and *National Geographic* is still widely enjoyed.

Art journals, perceived by some as worldly and immoral before the Civil War, also gained in popularity. Refinements in lithographic and photographic reproduction made it possible for Americans who had never set foot in an art gallery to see the work of artists like Currier and Ives in accurate detail. Journals devoted to music and theater also developed readerships in the late 19th century.

For those Americans who considered satire an art form, a humor magazine called *Puck* arrived in 1877. Edited by H. C. Bunner and illustrated by cartoonist Joseph Keppler, *Puck* dispensed laughter in weekly doses. In 1883, a few Harvard graduates sought to provide America with a highbrow journal of satire and criticism; the result was *Life* magazine.

Although black periodicals were few in number, most of them seemed to favor assimilation into white Euro-American culture. One black leader who disagreed vehemently was W. E. B. Du Bois (shown here), whose magazine, *The Crisis*, became the official publication of the National Association for the Advancement of Colored People (NAACP).

THE CRISIS

A RECORD OF THE DARKER RACES

Volume One   NOVEMBER, 1910   Number One

Edited by W. E. BURGHARDT DU BOIS, with the co-operation of Oswald Garrison Villard, J. Max Barber, Charles Edward Russell, Kelly Miller, W. S. Braithwaite and M. D. Maclean.

CONTENTS

Along the Color Line   3

Opinion   7

Editorial   10

The N. A. A. C. P.   12

Athens and Browns-
ville   13
By MOORFIELD STOREY

The Burden   14

What to Read   15

PUBLISHED MONTHLY BY THE

National Association for the Advancement of Colored People

AT TWENTY VESEY STREET   NEW YORK CITY

ONE DOLLAR A YEAR   TEN CENTS A COPY

Du Bois juggled magazine publishing with his duties as a college professor. *The Crisis* (shown here) was filled with articles supporting his demand for black civil rights.

New Audiences, New Magazines

Although most magazine publishers of the 1800s were white males, blacks and women also made their mark. The few black periodicals in print before 1865 were obliterated by the Civil War, but the ones that emerged during the Reconstruction reiterated the call for equal rights. Some black magazines, like the *A.M.E. Church Review*, were funded by a church and edited by ministers. Founded in 1884, the *A.M.E. Church Review* survived well into the 20th century. When two schoolteachers started *Southland* in 1890, it was the first black periodical published in the South.

Black periodicals were a forum for opposing views. Most publishers seemed to advocate accommodation as espoused by Booker T. Washington, who believed that the best way for blacks to conquer prejudice was to gradually assimilate themselves into white culture. W. E. B. Du Bois, on the other hand, saw accommodation as a sure ticket to second-class citizenship. After becoming a professor at Atlanta University, Du Bois launched a few of his own magazines in the early twentieth century. Among them were *Crisis: A Record of the Darker Races* and *Horizon: A Journal of Color*. In these and other magazines, Du Bois wrote that blacks needed to defend their rights and to actively protest the multitude of injustices they still faced despite Emancipation.

Another group long unrecognized by the magazine industry was women. In the late 1800s, however, publishers began to notice the increasing number of feminine names on their subscription lists. Soon, entire magazines—many edited by women—emerged to rally readers around the issue of women's rights. The right to vote was of particular interest, as demonstrated by the publication of *Revolution*, a journal founded in 1868 by Susan B. Anthony and Elizabeth Cady Stanton.

Other suffrage magazines, like Lucy Stone's more conservative *Women's Journal*, soon followed. As the movement reached a fever pitch, anti-suffragists responded with magazines like *True Woman*, which urged women to remain content with the rights they had.

The interests of all women—regardless of their political leanings—were reflected in mass-marketed periodicals. Some, such as the 1870 *Chicago Magazine of Fashion, Music and Home Reading*, were published and edited exclusively by women. Female-run magazines didn't meet with much support from the male-dominated publishing community. But the publication of fashion magazines often entailed cooperation between the sexes, with men handling the business of production while women oversaw editorial content. Two notable examples were *Harper's Bazar: A Repository of Fashion, Pleasure and Instruction*, first published in 1867 with Mary L. Booth in the editor's chair, and *Vogue*, started in 1892 under the editorship of Josephine Redding.

One of the best-known women's magazines of all time, *Ladies' Home Journal* was the result of husband-wife collaboration. In 1879, Cyrus K. Curtis started an agricultural journal in Philadelphia called *Tribune and Farmer*. Although his magazine included a household hints column for farmers' wives, Curtis's own wife, Louisa Knapp, was quick to point out its shortcomings. Mrs. Curtis took over the column, renaming it "Women and the Home" and filling it with her own brand of domestic wisdom. By 1883, his wife's column was so popular that Curtis issued it as a separate monthly supplement. This supplement grew into an altogether new magazine.

The newly titled *Ladies' Home Journal* was filled with household hints, recipes, and fashion tips and boasted a circulation of 20,000. While his wife edited, Curtis secured the bylines of great women

Early magazine publishers virtually ignored women. Susan B. Anthony (shown here) and Elizabeth Cady Stanton sought to remedy this when they founded *Revolution* in 1868. With its focus on promoting women's suffrage, *Revolution* paved the way for like-minded magazines as well as publications opposing the suffrage movement.

writers of the day, such as Louisa May Alcott, and made sure the magazine was liberally sprinkled with advertising. The Curtises would be proud to know that *Ladies' Home Journal* is alive and well today — and that even a century later, the format they pioneered has not changed much.

The Telegraph and the Telephone

BEFORE THE INVENTION OF THE TELEGRAPH IN THE 19TH century, long-distance communication depended entirely on transportation. Information—mail, books, newspapers, magazines— could be transmitted only as fast as the people, horses, or vehicles that carried it. But the discovery in 1820 of the electromagnetic field made possible a revolution in communications technology.

While experimenting in Copenhagen, Hans Christian Oersted, a Danish physicist, discovered that by connecting a battery to a wire loop, he could make the needle of a compass move—even though the compass was not touching the battery or the wires. The energy that moved the compass needle became known as the electromagnetic field. Electromagnetic energy was the basis for the development of all telecommunications.

Communication

Telephone and telegraph wires weave a net over Lower Broadway in 1889. Major cities already had large amounts of telegraph wire hanging by end of the 1870s, when telephone service became possible. As telephone companies scrambled to meet the demands of their urban customers, the resulting tangle of old and new wires created chaos overhead.

THE TELEGRAPH

In theory, the telegraph was a giant electromagnet: if a wire was looped between two distant points, a battery wired to one of these points could send its energy to the other. In 1837, William Cooke and Charles Wheatstone applied this theory when they patented a five-needle telegraph and installed a line along the Great Western Railway in England.

In America, a literature professor named Samuel Finley Breese Morse became interested in electromagnetic energy after a visit to Europe and invented a telegraph receiver. His invention consisted of an electromagnet attached to a pen, which marked a piece of paper when someone operated a switch at the other end of a telegraph line. To produce readable messages, Morse had to invent a system of dots and dashes to represent numerals and the letters of the alphabet. On May 24, 1844, the first Morse code telegram shot from Baltimore to Washington along a telegraph line. The message was dramatic—"What hath God wrought?"

Telegraph companies soon sprang up almost everywhere. Most were consolidated into the Western Union Telegraph Company in 1865. One year later, Western Union boasted 2,250 offices and had bedecked the landscape with over 100,000 miles of telegraph wire. In 1866, the first Transatlantic Telegraph Cable also went into operation. In less than 50 years, the electromagnetic field had been transformed from a scientific principle into a quick, practical way of sending messages across oceans.

THE TELEPHONE

The future king of telecommunications was still a teenager when transatlantic telegraph service came into being. Alexander Graham Bell

This painting re-creates the scene of Alexander Graham Bell's first success with the telephone. History holds that Bell, who accidentally spilled some acid on his clothing, summoned Watson (in doorway) over a telephone prototype—and that his young assistant heard him clearly.

was born in Edinburgh, Scotland, in 1847. His father, Alexander Melville Bell, was a professor of elocution who developed Visible Speech, a code of written symbols representing speech sounds. Visible Speech won Melville Bell wide acclaim in Europe and America, but he ended up moving his family to Canada in 1870 after one of his sons died of tuberculosis.

Bell's surviving son and namesake, Alexander, moved from Canada to New England in 1871 to give a series of lectures on the education of the deaf. The following year, he set up the School of Vocal Physiology in Boston. In 1873, he further followed in his father's footsteps by becoming a professor of vocal physiology and elocution at Boston University. One of his deaf students, Mabel Hubbard, was the daughter of Gardiner Greene Hubbard, the wealthy lawyer who founded *National Geographic* magazine. Bell would go on to marry Mabel Hubbard, and her father would become his financial backer.

Financial backing was important to Bell because he had been developing an invention called the harmonic telegraph, which would be able to send several telegraphic messages at a time across a single wire. Tuning forks on both the sending and receiving ends of the wire would convert electromagnetic impulses into sounds. Bell was inspired by Hermann von Helmholtz, a German scientist who had worked on producing vowel sounds through electrical tuning forks. He was able to personally examine von Helmholtz's device when fellow scientists at the Massachusetts Institute of Technology granted him access to their state-of-the-art facilities. But Bell realized that if he wanted to perfect his harmonic telegraph, he would need a mechanically gifted assistant.

Bell found such an assistant in Thomas A. Watson. Watson was born in Salem, Massachusetts, in 1854 and had a strong background in

Bell's exhibitor's pass for the 1876 Centennial Exposition in Philadelphia. So impressed by the telephone was one of the exposition's judges, Lord Kelvin, that he collaborated with Bell to perfect it.

Communication

This drawing depicts the first telephone conversation between Salem and Boston, which took place before a Salem audience on February 12, 1877. Bell had just been awarded a patent for his box telephone (inset) on January 30.

electrical machinery even though he was very young. Bell and Watson started their collaboration in the shop where Watson was employed. On June 2, 1875, they made an important discovery by accident. Watson was tuning the magnetic reeds of the telegraph to harmonize with Bell's reeds. When he plucked one of the reeds, the sound was clearly transmitted to Bell, who was in another room. Within one day of this breakthrough, the duo had sketched plans for the first true telephone. This prototype was patented on March 7, 1876, but it wasn't until March 10 that the first sentence was successfully transmitted by telephone.

On that day, Bell accidentally spilled sulfuric acid on his clothing while experimenting with a battery-powered telephone. Watson was able to hear Bell's now-famous call, "Mr. Watson, come here, I want you!" from another part of the laboratory.

The partners developed short-distance outdoor lines that spring, and when the Centennial Exposition—an exhibition of the latest innovations in art, science, and technology—opened on May 10, 1876, Bell's telephone was there. This was at the urging of Gardiner Greene Hubbard, who was one of the Exposition's organizers.

Bell was right to comply with his future father-in-law's request, because the distinguished physicist Lord Kelvin, who was present to judge the newest electrical inventions, declared the telephone the most wonderful device he had seen in America. That July, Kelvin began working with Bell in his Boston laboratory. The excitement proved too much for the young inventor, however, and he retreated to Canada.

Fortunately, Bell soon returned to Watson and the Boston laboratory to perfect his creation. On October 9, 1876, they successfully completed a two-way call using the telegraphy lines between Boston and Cambridgeport. Bell described that day as the proudest in his life, "marking the successful completion of Telephony," although "much doubtless remains to be done in perfecting the details of the apparatus." To that end, Watson made improvements that enhanced the telephone's power and clarity, and he and Bell completed a call between Boston and Salem—a distance of 16 miles.

On January 30, 1877, Bell was awarded a patent for his new "box telephone," a single unit that both transmitted and received calls, powered by a durable magnet instead of a battery.

"UNIVERSAL SERVICE"

It was time to market this technological wonder. That spring, Bell presented almost vaudevillian shows that touted "The Miracle, Wonderful Discovery of the Age" in New York, Boston, and Providence, Rhode Island. Before captivated audiences in rented halls, Bell would telephone Watson, who stood by in the Boston laboratory. Watson, who sang and played loud recorded music, was sometimes too noisy for his neighbors' comfort, so he created the first "telephone booth," which was nothing more than blankets thrown around barrel hoops. This makeshift shelter soundproofed Watson as he belted out his routine.

The extravaganzas paid off. Bell and Hubbard decided to use their profits to implement a complete system of telephone service, rather than randomly selling individual units. While the newly married Bell honeymooned in Europe with Mabel Hubbard in late 1877, her father and Watson toiled at systematizing the telephone industry. Hubbard set up the Bell Telephone Company in July, and by November there were 3,000 Bell telephones in service.

Bell Telephone faced competition in its quest to speed communication, though. The Western Union Telegraph Company was selling telephones

Mabel Hubbard Bell and Alexander Graham Bell with their children, Elsie and Marian. This family picture was taken in 1885, before Bell's patents expired, leaving the field of telecommunications open to small, independent companies eager to cash in on his invention.

Communication

Switchboard operators patch together a veritable spider-web of telephone wire. The first operators had to use customer names to connect callers. Life got slightly easier for them after 1880, when a doctor in Lowell, Massachusetts, developed the first system of telephone numbers to expedite the placement of calls.

designed by Thomas Edison and Elisha Gray—a rival inventor whom Bell had narrowly beaten in the patent race. In September of 1878 Bell Telephone Company filed a suit alleging that Western Union was in violation of patent laws. Bell won the case, but the enterprise he originated would be dogged by imitators for years to come. By 1880, Bell Telephone would buy out Western Union's phone lines and become American Bell.

After Bell's patents expired in the mid-1890s, independent phone companies sprang up to capitalize on his revolutionary invention. The industry became a jumble of disjointed services as more and more small companies crowded the market. The Bell organization faltered under pressure from the competition until Theodore N. Vail returned as general manager in 1907, after having left American Bell 20 years earlier because of conflict with then-president William Forbes.

In 1908, Vail breathed new life into Bell and its subsidiary, AT&T (American Telephone and Telegraph) with the slogan, "One Policy—One System, Universal Service." Further stressing the need for "universal service," one advertisement counseled prospective customers that the Bell system was no more of a monopoly than was the nation's postal service. Another explained that the telephone's usefulness lay not in the instrument itself, but in the network of "twenty million voices" that a Bell telephone could access, "ready for you to call up day or night."

In 1909, Vail acquired the Western Union Telegraph Company, which Bell had successfully sued back in 1878, because he believed that a combined telegraph and telephone company would epitomize "universal service." Vail resurrected Western Union's 25,000 ailing franchises by consolidating them with Bell. Advertising copy now boasted, "When you lift the receiver of a Bell Telephone and call Western Union you are in communication with the world."

As the first decade of the 20th century came to an end, Americans could share information and ideas amongst themselves and with the entire world—sometimes, in a matter of minutes. The ongoing search for new and better ways of communicating has yielded the fax machine and electronic mail in recent years. This search will no doubt continue, with ever more amazing results.

FURTHER READING

Barmeier, Jim. *Manners and Customs*. New York: Chelsea House Publishers, 1997.

Boettinger, Henry M. *The Telephone Book: Bell, Watson, Vail and American Life* 1876–1983. rev. ed. New York: Stearn Publishers Ltd., 1983.

Brooks, John. *Telephone: The First Hundred Years*. New York: Harper & Row, 1976.

Fisher, Leonard Everett. *The Newspapers*. Illustrated by the author. New York: Holiday House, 1981.

Fuller, Wayne F. *The American Mail: Enlarger of the Common Life*. Chicago: University of Chicago Press, 1985.

Ritchie, David. *Frontier Life*. New York: Chelsea House Publishers, 1996.

Sterling, Christopher H., and George Shiers, eds. *Telephone: An Historical Anthology*. reprint. Salem, N.Y.: Ayer Co., 1976.

Tebbel, John. *Between Covers: The Rise and Transformation of Book Publishing in America*. New York: Oxford University Press, 1987.

Tebbel, John, and Mary Ellen Zuckerman. *The Magazine in America: 1741–1990*. New York: Oxford University Press, 1991.

INDEX

PICTURE CREDITS

Every effort has been made to contact the copyright owners of photographs and illustrations used in this book. In the event that the holder of a copyright has not heard from us, he or she should contact Chelsea House Publishers.

GERALDINE GAN is a writer and editor living in New York. Her publications include the Chelsea House book *Lives of Asian Americans: Arts, Entertainment, Sports.*

.